COLONIAL PEOPLE

The Doctor

KATIE MARSICO

 **Marshall Cavendish**
Benchmark
New York

Other Marshall Cavendish Offices:

Marshall Cavendish International (Asia) Private Limited, 1 New Industrial Road, Singapore 536196 • Marshall Cavendish
International (Thailand) Co Ltd., 253 Asoke, 12th Flr, Sukhumvit 21 Road, Klongtoey Nua, Wattana, Bangkok 10110,
Thailand • Marshall Cavendish (Malaysia) Sdn Bhd, Times Subang, Lot 46, Subang Hi-Tech Industrial Park, Batu Tiga,
40000 Shah Alam, Selangor Darul Ehsan, Malaysia

Marshall Cavendish is a trademark of Times Publishing Limited

All websites were available and accurate when this book was sent to press.

Library of Congress Cataloging-in-Publication Data

Marsico, Katie, 1980–
The doctor / Katie Marsico.
p. cm. — (Colonial people)
Includes index.
Summary: "Explore the life of a colonial doctor and his importance to the
community, as well as everyday life, responsibilities, and social practices
during that time"—Provided by publisher.
ISBN 978-1-60870-412-5 (print)
ISBN 978-1-60870-636-5 (e-book)
1. Physicians—United States—History—17th century—Juvenile literature.
2. Physicians—United States—History—18th century—Juvenile literature.
3. Medicine—United States—History—17th century—Juvenile literature.
4. Medicine—United States—History—18th century—Juvenile literature.
5. United States—History—Colonial period, ca. 1600–1775—Juvenile literature.
I. Title.
R152.M26 2012
610.69'5097309033—dc22
2010033895

Editor: Joy Bean
Publisher: Michelle Bisson
Art Director: Anahid Hamparian
Series Designer: Kay Petronio

Expert Reader: Paul Douglas Newman, Ph.D., Department of History, University of Pittsburgh at Johnstown

Photo research by Marybeth Kavanagh

Cover photo by Frans van Mieris/The Bridgeman Art Library/Getty Images
The photographs in this book are used by permission and through the courtesy of: North Wind Picture Archives: 4, 18;
The Granger Collection, NYC: 8, 20; The Image Works: Dinodia: 10; Mary Evans Picture Library, 17; ullstein-Archiv
Gerstenberg, 24; Sueddeutsche Zeitung Photo, 32; The Colonial Williamsburg Foundation: 11; Special Collections,
John D. Rockefeller, Jr. Library, 27; SuperStock: Science and Society, 15; The Bridgeman Art Library: Massachusetts
Historical Society, Boston, MA, USA, 26; Getty Images: MPI, 34, 36, 40, 42; Stock Montage, 44.

Printed in Malaysia (T)
1 3 5 6 4 2

CONTENTS

ONE

Hard Work in a New World

Thomas Wotton faced a difficult task when he arrived in the British colony of Virginia in April 1607. Wotton was a doctor who had traveled from Great Britain to Jamestown, his country's first permanent settlement in North America. He lived and worked alongside men such as the famous explorer Captain John Smith. Wotton soon discovered, however, that healing the sick and keeping people well at Jamestown would challenge his skills and knowledge.

In 1607, about 105 settlers landed on Virginia's shores. They were not used to the weather and geography of North America's eastern coast. Summers were hot and humid, while winters were damp and chilly. As a result of exposure to this new climate, many of the colonists became sick or suffered from conditions such as heatstroke.

The first colonists arrive at Jamestown in 1607.

The settlers also caught a variety of deadly diseases that spread quickly throughout the region's swamps. Ailments such as **malaria** and **dysentery** killed many of the Jamestown colonists. Poor nutrition weakened their bodies and made them even more vulnerable to these illnesses. Starvation was also a serious and constant threat. For men like Wotton, treating the sick was no easy task.

Captain Smith praised Wotton's efforts. In one account, Smith noted that several of the settlers overcame diseases thanks to the "[skillful] diligence of Mr. Thomas Wotton our Chirurgian generall [surgeon general]." Yet Smith also observed that the colonists were plagued "with such famine and sicknes [sickness] that the living were scarce able to bury the dead." This statement was no exaggeration. Only 38 of the original 105 Jamestown settlers survived the winter of 1607 to 1608.

Wotton was among the survivors, but he soon returned to Europe. Though he was one of colonial America's first doctors, he would not be the last. It would be nearly 168 years before the colonies won their independence from Great Britain to become the United States. In that time, hundreds of thousands of men, women, and children traveled to colonial America from Europe and Africa.

Some settlers came against their will aboard slave ships that sailed from African shores. Others made the long ocean voyage from Europe in search of religious freedom. Many individuals journeyed to the colonies in the hopes of building their fortunes or making a fresh start in a new land. During that period, the role of doctors grew, changed, and shaped everyday life for the colonists who settled America.

Early Medical Experts and Common Cures

In addition to Wotton, a handful of other colonists who had experience practicing medicine left Great Britain to cross the Atlantic Ocean in the seventeenth century. These men and women did their best to care for sick settlers so that the British colonies in North America would prosper and grow. Some of them had a good deal of experience, as they had worked as physicians and surgeons in their homeland.

At that time, physicians were university-educated men who had studied **anatomy** and **botany**. They diagnosed medical conditions and recommended treatments. People generally looked upon surgeons as working-class laborers who trained with physicians. They could handle a knife well enough to perform surgical procedures such as **amputations**.

A doctor studies blood he has drained from one of his patients in an attempt to cure her sickness.

Seventeenth-century colonists claimed other types of medical backgrounds as well. Some of these individuals were not technically doctors, yet they had the same responsibilities as modern members of the medical profession. Apothecaries were druggists who made medicines from chemicals and plants. Midwives were women who cared for pregnant patients and delivered their babies.

Even barbers and tailors practiced medicine from time to time, bleeding sick customers or stitching open wounds.

Bleeding, or bloodletting, was a common medical procedure until the 1800s. It was rooted in the belief that a person's health depended on the balance of four bodily fluids, or humors. Early doctors thought that a person who had too much of one humor could become sick. Their solution was often to bleed a patient by applying bloodsucking **leeches** or making cuts with a small surgical knife called a lancet.

Doctors hoped that draining unnecessary fluids from a person's body would restore the balance of the humors and cure the illness. In many cases, though, this "cure" created even more problems for the patient. People who were already sick often became weaker when they lost blood.

Seventeenth-century doctors did not always offer their patients bad advice. For example, they attempted to balance bodily humors through other methods, such as blowing one's nose, **sweating**, and using **emetics**. Ultimately, nose blowing helped prevent respiratory infections, sweating often reduced fevers, and emetics sometimes relieved stomach problems.

When patients survived their illnesses as a result of such techniques, they were grateful for what they felt was valuable

Medicine Based on Walnuts and Beans

Seventeenth-century doctors did not always use bleeding to address a person's medical complaints. Many believed that their patients should eat foods that looked like whatever part of the body was bothering them. So, if a patient said that her head ached, a physician might tell her to snack on walnuts, which resemble small human brains. Doctors also advised patients with kidney problems to eat kidney beans. Early doctors reasoned that the beans were so similar to the body part that they simply had to be part of the cure!

medical wisdom. Yet many people also thought they had been spared death thanks to the strength of their religious faith. Hundreds of years ago, it was not uncommon for people to believe that sickness was God's punishment for human sinfulness, and that survival was a sign of God's forgiveness.

Coping with Life in the Colonies

Seventeenth-century medical experts had a limited understanding of the human body, so they were not always able to heal their patients. Many people died from sicknesses that doctors easily treat today with modern medicines and cures. Saving lives was an intense challenge for doctors working in America during the 1600s.

Leeches feed on the blood of whatever person or animal they latch onto.

For starters, early colonists faced a shortage of medical experts. Doctors who decided to brave a new life in the colonies often did not stay for long. Some preferred to return to Europe, which was generally considered a far more civilized continent than the wild and mysterious North America. Many physicians thought that England and nearby countries were also better locations to study the latest medical theories and techniques.

Others simply decided that taking care of the American colonists was too dangerous and exhausting. The harsh winters along the northeastern coast, as well as the smothering humidity of southern coastal swamplands, greatly increased settlers' risks of becoming ill. The colonists' lack of familiarity with their new continent did not help, either.

Settlers often drank from rivers and streams that were filled with unhealthy **bacteria**. They also suffered from poor nutrition and starvation. This was partially because they did not automatically know which fruits, vegetables, and grains grew well in American soil or which local forests were best for hunting.

Physical exhaustion and conflicts with American Indians took a toll on the colonists, too. These stresses added to the many circumstances that made them easy targets for poor health. Malaria, yellow fever, typhoid fever, **smallpox**, and dysentery regularly sickened or killed early settlers in America. Cholera, pneumonia, and scarlet fever were other common ailments. Sometimes certain illnesses spread through a colony so quickly that they caused a medical **epidemic**.

Such situations placed doctors in great demand. Yet it was nearly impossible for the limited number of physicians and surgeons who arrived from Great Britain to satisfy the medical needs of all the early colonists. As more European settlers and

African slaves started moving to America during the 1600s, they began spreading out across the eastern part of the continent.

Since there were few medical experts among them, patients often treated their own health problems as best they could. After all, it could take an entire day on horseback to summon the local doctor! The situation gradually started to improve as British settlers developed stronger and more stable communities in colonial America.

TWO

Medical Treatments and Training

During the late 1600s, colonists built several towns and cities along North America's Atlantic coast. They eventually learned how to survive in their new land. Yet colonial doctors still faced many dangers and challenges. During the 1600s, life expectancy for people worldwide was shorter than it is today. But North American colonists struggled with additional problems that further shortened their lives.

What tools and methods did colonial doctors rely upon to treat these settlers? Bleeding, sweating, and the use of emetics remained popular healing techniques. But colonial medicine included more methods than bloodsucking leeches and mixtures that made people vomit. For example, doctors frequently recommended that their patients use a poultice to heal sores or to ease body aches. To make this medical dressing, they would heat a soft substance such as bread meal or clay and then spread

Surviving Surgery in Colonial Times

If colonists had more serious complaints than a slight fever or occasional aches and pains, doctors sometimes performed surgery. The success rates for complex medical operations were low during early colonial times. For example, historians estimate that only about one in four people survived any kind of surgical amputation.

Surgery was risky because seventeenth-century doctors did not understand the importance of properly sterilizing their hands and medical equipment. They unknowingly spread germs, which often caused fatal infections. Other times, for different reasons, doctors stood by helplessly as their patients died from blood loss and shock. Either way, colonial operating tables frequently posed just as many dangers and risks as the ailments that brought sick colonists there in the first place.

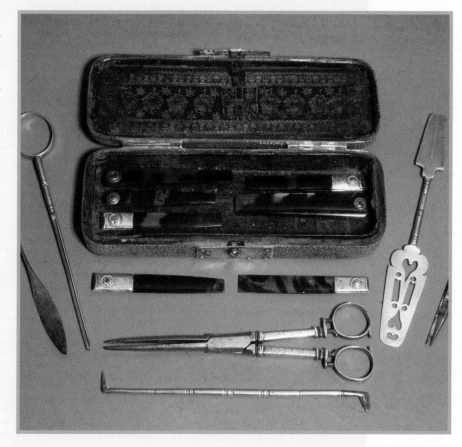

it on a cloth. The patient placed the cloth on whatever part of his or her body was hurting. Sometimes colonial cures were even simpler. When patients complained of fever, doctors usually advised them to wipe themselves with a cold rag to bring down their temperatures.

Learning from Local Peoples

Doctors working in America during the late 1600s did not have all the answers to preventing and curing diseases. Yet this did not stop them from trying to learn more about the new land around them so they could use it to produce new medicines. For thousands of years, humans had been experimenting with **herbs**—the stems, leaves, and roots of various plants—in an effort to develop more effective medical treatments. Colonial doctors brought some of these remedies with them when they arrived on American shores.

For example, doctors believed that smoking an herb called rosemary in a pipe would help cure coughs and lung diseases. Some medical experts used dried marigold flowers to treat patients with heart problems. Others prepared teas from ginger and chamomile to soothe upset stomachs.

After arriving in the colonies, doctors were eager to find new herbs and plants to improve their medicine chests. Yet it was not always easy to determine which plants would best serve this

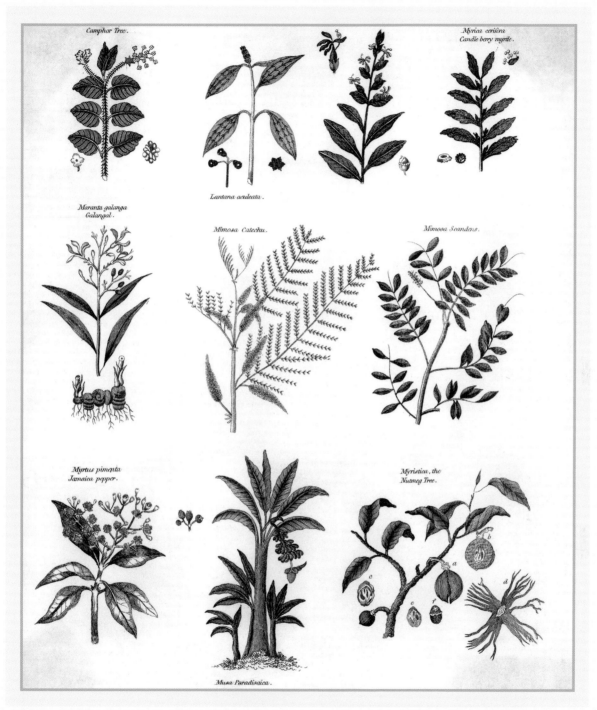

This sketch of commonly used herbs dates back to the 1700s. Some of the herbs pictured include pepper, nutmeg, and camphor.

purpose. Luckily for the colonists, however, local American Indian tribes also had been studying their natural surroundings for centuries.

American Indians relied on the wisdom of shamans, or medicine men. Their healing practices often involved religious rituals such as dancing and chanting. For this reason, some colonial doctors had little respect for the shamans' ideas, which they felt were based more on magic than on medical wisdom.

On the other hand, many colonists gradually came to appreciate the American Indians' knowledge of herbs and plants that would help cure their ailments. For instance, some colonial doctors'

Shamans often wore special ceremonial robes and headdresses when they danced as part of healing rituals.

journals reveal that they used different parts of dogwood trees to make medicines to treat fevers. Some also created mixtures with goldthread flowers to ease the pain of patients who complained of sore mouths. It is likely that the doctors borrowed these healing techniques from their American Indian neighbors.

Preparing to Practice Colonial Medicine

In addition to observing the practices of American Indian tribes, colonial doctors learned new skills in other ways. Most did not train and build their careers like today's medical experts do. During the late 1600s, few formal medical schools existed in Europe, and there were absolutely none in the colonies.

For this reason, some colonists decided to return to their homelands across the Atlantic Ocean to attend medical schools. There they could learn about the latest advances in anatomy and botany. Once students completed their education, though, they often chose to remain in Europe. Not everyone was prepared to face the challenges of surviving in the colonies—let alone practicing medicine there!

Colonists who wanted to become physicians had a few other educational alternatives. Some young men were able to take anatomy classes at new schools in the Northeast, such as Harvard

College in Cambridge, Massachusetts. But these students did not receive the detailed and lengthy training that modern medical students do. Such educational programs simply were not available during this period of history.

Most colonists who were interested in practicing medicine developed their skills by working as apprentices. This means they studied under someone who was already an expert in the field of medicine. Colonists trained for many other trades in a similar manner. Everyone from blacksmiths to printers gained skills and experience by working as apprentices.

During colonial times, some Europeans trained at teaching clinics such as the one shown here in Paris, France.

In colonial America, medical apprentices often lived with the doctors who were training them. They usually ran errands and performed household chores for their teachers, who were sometimes called masters. In return, doctors allowed their apprentices to watch them treat patients and prepare medicines. They also shared with students their knowledge of anatomy and botany, along with whatever medical books and equipment they owned.

Once a physician, surgeon, apothecary, or midwife believed an apprentice had learned enough skills to practice medicine independently, the master released the apprentice from service. Sometimes a master provided his or her former apprentice with a few tools of the trade and announced to the public that the person was ready to treat patients. In other cases, apprentices decided on their own that they were prepared to work alone and simply declared themselves to be doctors.

There was no set number of years that early colonists had to train in order to claim that they were ready to treat patients. Nor were there any exams they had to pass to demonstrate their knowledge or abilities. Thus, colonists who chose to enter the field of medicine were held to few professional standards. This reality affected the way patients viewed their colonial doctors, as well doctors' effectiveness in caring for their communities.

THREE

Doctors' Roles in Colonial Communities

Neither overseas study nor work as an apprentice could guarantee that a colonial doctor would be skilled, responsible, or well suited to his career. Some of the individuals who practiced medicine in the colonies were indeed talented, intelligent, and dedicated to helping their patients. Others, however, were more interested in charging colonists high fees than in providing actual cures.

Starting in the 1630s, colonists in Virginia passed a few laws in an effort to **regulate** the practice of medicine. Colonial leaders demanded that "physicians and surgeons . . . declare on Oath the value of their Medicine." Lawmakers hoped that doctors would take their responsibilities more seriously if they faced the threat of imprisonment.

Such rules were difficult to enforce, however. It was hard for patients to prove that a doctor had not done his job properly. In the meantime, medical experts often demanded high fees that they were legally entitled to collect even if a person died under their care.

Some early colonial leaders tried to limit the fees doctors could charge based on their level of education and experience. Yet this strategy proved even a greater challenge for American colonists than for Europeans. In England, for example, physicians demanded higher fees than surgeons did because physicians attended classes at universities and received more formal medical training. In the colonies, however, the differences between physicians and surgeons were less obvious. Doctors' skills and levels of experience were so varied that it was hard to know if they were charging fair rates or if they were truly capable of caring for the sick.

People of Many Professions

A shortage of labor in the colonies affected the role that medical experts played in seventeenth-century America. Many colonists who trained and worked as doctors had to perform more than one job in their communities. For instance, in the northeastern colonies, several doctors also served as **clergymen**. Medical professionals

It was not uncommon for colonial patients to receive medical treatment in one room while someone got a shave or a haircut in the next! This was because barbers often practiced medicine as well.

who had been lucky enough to study some anatomy or botany at European universities or early American colleges frequently doubled as teachers.

A settler named John Winthrop II is one of the most famous examples of a colonial doctor who held several different jobs in his community. Winthrop lived and worked in Massachusetts and Connecticut from 1631 to 1676. During that time, he was widely recognized for his skills as a lawyer and scientist. Winthrop was also deeply involved in politics in Connecticut, of which he eventually became governor.

Winthrop also led a busy life as a colonial doctor. According to some historical sources, he saw an average of twelve patients a day and cared for approximately five hundred families by traveling throughout Connecticut. Winthrop was committed to helping his colony grow and develop on many fronts. He proved this dedication time and again by not charging his patients for medical services.

Costly and Controversial Care

Early colonists greatly benefited from the care of doctors such as Winthrop. But tending to the settlers' medical needs was not Winthrop's only responsibility, and he could not be everywhere in the colony at once. More important, not all colonial doctors were willing or able to offer their services for free.

Some doctors charged high fees in the hopes of building their fortunes in America. Others used their profits to ship medical supplies across the Atlantic Ocean from Europe. In addition, many doctors could not ignore the expenses that

Learning from Letters

Like many seventeenth-century colonial doctors, John Winthrop II tried to stay informed about the most recent advances in medicine by exchanging letters with other men of science. In those days, there were no telephones, radios, televisions, or computers. Instead, people like Winthrop kept journals and wrote letters that recorded their achievements, experiences, and countless questions. One letter that Winthrop received from a fellow colonist reveals a few of the herbs and plants that colonial doctors used to treat their patients.

"[I] have s ent [sent] you of all I have, or what I can get," wrote John Endicott, who was both an early governor of Massachusetts and something of a physician to settlers in that area. "Syrup of Violetts [violets], Sirrup [syrup] of Roses, Spirits of Mint, Spirits of Annis [anise], as you may see written upon the severall [several] vials. . . ." Since it was often difficult to obtain supplies from Europe, colonial physicians and surgeons sometimes shared chemicals, herbs, plants, and equipment in addition to exchanging medical knowledge.

A colonial apothecary relied upon this account book during the 1700s as a way to keep track of what patients owed him for his services.

arose from constantly traveling around the colonies to treat patients. Physicians, surgeons, apothecaries, and midwives were professionals who expected to earn a living based on the services they provided.

Regardless of why doctors charged fees, the cost of health care partly shaped how colonists viewed people in this line of work. On the one hand, several colonial physicians were well-respected

Grow Your Own Herb Garden

Starting in the 1600s, colonial doctors and their patients often grew herbs for medicinal purposes. Many modern-day Americans keep similar gardens today. You can plant your own herb garden by following the directions below.

You Will Need

- the seeds of four herbs of your choice
- a pen or pencil
- four index cards
- tape
- four small gardening pots
- potting soil
- a journal or notebook
- a ruler
- crayons or markers

Instructions

1. Decide which four herbs you want to plant, and purchase packets of seeds from your local hardware or gardening store. Below are a few suggested herbs, along with the various ailments that colonial doctors believed the herbs cured.

   basil—nervousness and eye problems
   dill—stomach troubles
   lavender—nervousness and sleeplessness
   oregano—joint pains and stomach troubles
   parsley—stomach troubles and skin wounds
   sage—headaches and fever

2. Carefully read the back of each seed packet to determine how much sunlight the different herbs need to grow. Find clean, flat surfaces where your plants can receive this amount of light on a daily basis. (Shelves or countertops near or in front of windows are often good spots.)

3. Using a pen or a pencil, label four index cards with the names of the herbs you have chosen. Tape a card to the outside of each gardening pot.

4. Fill each pot with potting soil, and plant and water your seeds according to the directions on the packets.

5. As your herbs grow, record your observations in a journal or notebook. Use a ruler to measure your plants, and use crayons or markers to draw pictures of them. Do not try to make your own medicines, but do ask an adult if any of your plants might be helpful in the kitchen. Some of the same herbs that doctors relied on to create colonial medicines can also add flavor to food!

members of their communities. Some had a considerable amount of wealth and influence among early British settlers. In many cases, these doctors were the same individuals who held important positions within local churches, businesses, and governments.

On the other hand, struggling colonists often thought twice about calling on doctors when they got sick because of the cost.

For settlers who were trying to build stable homes, shops, and farms, extra expenses were a hardship. Several colonists also felt it was not worth waiting for a doctor to travel long distances to reach them. Finally, colonists tended to fear medical treatments such as bleeding. From their point of view, a doctor's "cure" was frequently worse than whatever illnesses were bothering them!

For these reasons, colonists tended to rely heavily on friends, neighbors, and family members to nurse them through periods of sickness. They also used books called herbals in much the same way that we browse cookbooks for recipes today. Herbals contained directions for creating teas, poultices, and potions from plants, trees, herbs, and animal parts. These items served as cheap homemade medicines.

When colonists were ill, they consulted their trusted herbals to avoid the cost—and potential pain—of an expert's treatment. But this approach to healing did not last—and neither did colonists' negative attitude toward doctors. As the 1700s dawned, people who practiced medicine in America found themselves at the center of exciting and important advances in both science and colonial life.

FOUR

Eighteenth-Century Achievements

By the early 1700s, the colonies were not limited to a few scattered British settlements along the Atlantic coast. Hundreds of thousands of people lived and worked in America's fruitful farmlands and bustling towns and villages. They also flocked to rapidly growing colonial cities like Boston, New York City, and Philadelphia.

Many colonists had roots in England, yet some came from other European nations, such as Scotland, Ireland, France, Holland, and Germany. In addition, hundreds of thousands of slaves from Africa and the West Indies arrived at North American ports along the Atlantic coast. From there, they were sold to white masters, who frequently forced them to work on large farms called plantations.

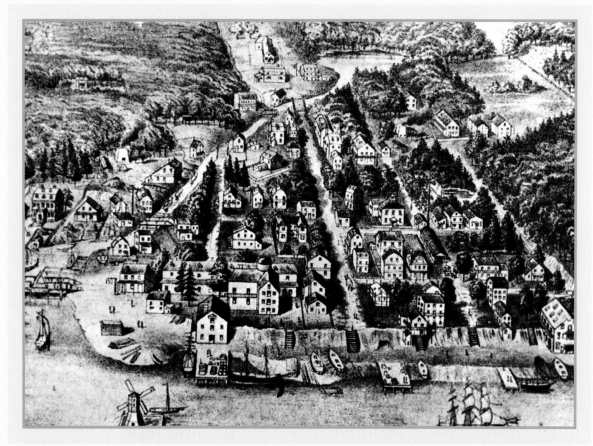

Philadelphia was a busy, crowded colonial city during the 1700s. It was also an important center of business and government activity.

This vast mixture of people, as well as the various types of work they did, were evidence of how much the colonies had grown since the early 1600s. Eighteenth-century colonists were still not in a position to take survival for granted, however. Epidemics continued to destroy colonial communities, and no one—including doctors—seemed to know how to stop them.

Smallpox and measles were common killers. Doctors and local authorities attempted to halt the spread of these diseases through quarantine laws. They tried to keep sick colonists separate from anyone who was at risk of catching their illnesses. In the end, though, such laws failed to eliminate the many epidemics that swept through the colonies.

Different Ideas about Inoculation

It was not until 1721 that a doctor from Boston asked colonists to consider a controversial new method of disease prevention. That year, Zabdiel Boylston responded to a local smallpox epidemic by **inoculating** nearly two hundred people. He performed this medical procedure by piercing a healthy patient's skin, taking pus from an infected person's smallpox sores, and placing the pus on the open wound he had created.

Boylston hoped that his patients would get a small, harmless dose of the disease. This would prepare their bodies to fight off the disease if they encountered it in the future, thus preventing them from becoming seriously ill and further spreading the epidemic. But not everyone was supportive of Boylston's techniques.

Medical experts and clergymen alike voiced their mistrust of inoculation. Many still subscribed to ancient medical ideas and thought that sickness was a punishment from heaven. They worried that inoculation challenged God's will. Boylston's critics also argued that the procedure might actually quicken the spread of smallpox and other diseases. Due to such fear and lack of understanding, Boylston and his supporters became targets of anger, threats, and even physical violence. However, the procedures were effective.

Boylston's success with inoculation eventually gained him fame in both America and Europe. It took several years for the majority of colonists to grasp the wisdom of his actions. Yet his work in 1721 led to important medical research on vaccination later in the century. It also influenced the way colonists viewed doctors and medicine in general.

Some colonists decided that it was time to open their minds to new ideas

An Hiftorical

ACCOUNT

OF THE

SMALL-POX

INOCULATED

IN

NEW ENGLAND,

Upon all Sorts of Perfons, *Whites*, *Blacks*, and of all Ages and Conftitutions.

With fome Account of the Nature of the Infection in the NATURAL and INOCULATED Way, and their different Effects on HUMAN BODIES.

With fome fhort DIRECTIONS to the UNEXPERIENCED in this Method of Practice.

Humbly dedicated to her Royal Highnefs the Princefs of WALES, by *Zabdiel Boylfton*, Phyfician.

LONDON:

Printed for S. CHANDLER, *at the* Crofs-Keys *in the* Poultry. M. DCC. XXVI.

The title page of a publication written by Boylston in 1726 that described his experiences with smallpox inoculation in colonial America.

about medical treatment. In Europe, a growing number of doctors were struggling to perfect their knowledge of anatomy, botany, and the use of herbs in medicines. Eighteenth-century Europeans still relied heavily on ancient beliefs, but their doctors were gradually approaching a set of medical practices that were based more on science than on superstition.

Setting New Standards

Life in America did not allow colonial doctors the same opportunities for research and learning that scientists in Europe had. Yet many slowly started accepting and appreciating the new knowledge and techniques that European medical experts shared with them. As a result, colonial doctors began to improve professional standards and patient care.

For instance, doctors formed the Medical Society of New Jersey in 1766. Before this point, there had been no real organization of colonial medical experts. Founders of the Medical Society of New Jersey said they hoped to "form a program embracing all the matters of highest concern to the profession: regulation of practice; educational standards for apprentices; fee schedules; and a code of ethics."

As time passed, similar groups sprang up throughout the colonies. Members pushed to hold medical professionals to

The First Colonial Hospital

In 1751, colonial doctor Thomas Bond teamed up with author, scientist, and politician Benjamin Franklin to create the first hospital in the American colonies. The pair founded Pennsylvania Hospital in Philadelphia to "care for the sick-poor and insane who were wandering the streets. . . ." Their achievement meant that local doctors could finally treat a large number of patients at a central location. This helped reduce the spread of disease and illness by giving sick colonists a place to rest and to receive immediate medical attention.

stricter standards. They worked to ensure that doctors charged fair fees. Members of some organizations started to insist that medical experts undergo a certain amount of training and pass specific exams before they could work as licensed professionals.

Colonists also began developing new ways for people to receive a formal medical education. In 1765, doctors John Morgan and William Shippen Jr., established the Medical School of the College of Philadelphia in Pennsylvania. It was the colonies' first official medical school. By that point, though, far more was changing in America than colonists' ideas about medicine and the people who practiced it. A political **revolution** was about to sweep through the colonies, and doctors were destined to play several important parts in it.

FIVE

Wounds and Wisdom During the War

The relationship between Great Britain's government and the American colonists had changed a great deal since the days Jamestown was founded, in the early 1600s. At first, the American colonists had been dependent on their parent country for money, goods, and supplies. As time passed, however, the colonists had become more independent.

New Americans managed successful farms and businesses. Many held important positions in their communities. These men and women were growing tired of British officials who interfered with day-to-day life in the colonies. They opposed the high taxes that King George III of Britain had levied. The colonists felt they had no voice in political and military happenings across the

Atlantic Ocean. Therefore they believed it was logical for British politicians and soldiers to keep out of their affairs in America.

King George and his countrymen disagreed, and the colonists ultimately had to fight a war to win their independence from Great Britain. This conflict became known as the American Revolutionary War (1776–1783). Yet soldiers and statesmen were not the war's only key players. Doctors had meaningful roles as well.

To begin with, four physicians signed the Declaration of Independence on July 4, 1776. This document officially announced the colonists' freedom from British rule. Doctors Benjamin Rush, Lyman Hall, Matthew Thornton, and Josiah Bartlett wrote their names on the declaration alongside those of other famous political leaders, such as Thomas Jefferson, John Adams, and Benjamin Franklin.

Struggling to Save Lives

As the Revolutionary War progressed, colonial surgeons and physicians found themselves doing far more than practicing their signatures. Bloody battles erupted all over the colonies, and soldiers fighting in the **Continental army** required constant and immediate medical care. Colonial leaders responded to their needs by forming a military medical department.

The Declaration of Independence reshaped America's identity as a nation. The war that followed also led to important and lasting changes in the way medicine was practiced there.

Doctors who served in the medical unit of the army faced incredible challenges. On the most basic level, military camps were filthy and lacked clean water, fresh food, and medical supplies. These camps were perfect places for diseases such as dysentery and smallpox to spread. In addition, soldiers' wounds easily became infected as a result of poor sanitation.

To make matters worse, colonial doctors had no **anesthetics** to offer their patients. This fact struck fear into the hearts of seriously wounded soldiers who faced amputation. Soldiers often had to bite down on wooden sticks or bullets to cope with the intense pain of medical procedures. As a result, colonial physicians and surgeons serving with the military medical department quickly became used to the sound of constant screaming.

Doctors who cared for the Continental army during the Revolutionary War also continued to struggle with a lack of knowledge and training. The practice of medicine had advanced since the early 1600s, but many doctors still relied on ancient beliefs rather than on newer, more controversial ideas. For instance, bleeding remained a popular practice, as did the notion that imbalances of bodily humors were the main causes of illness.

Doctors who served on the battlefield during the Revolutionary War had varied levels of training. Some had graduated from medical school, but others had barely completed apprenticeships. Several had read books about anatomy or botany but lacked any experience working on the human body. Historians estimate that about 1,200 doctors provided medical services to the Continental army, but only between 100 and 300 actually had medical degrees.

By the time the war ended, approximately 25,000 of the Revolution's 250,000 soldiers had died fighting for colonists' rights. The doctors who cared for these individuals were often

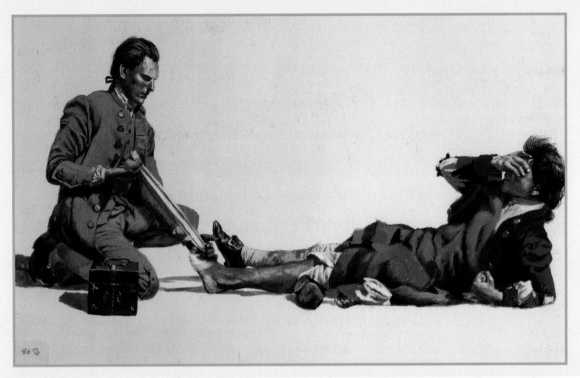

A colonial doctor bandages a soldier's foot with cloth from a tent during the Revolutionary War. Medical experts who treated members of the Continental army often had to make do with limited supplies.

tired and frustrated when they left their operating tables and hospital tents. Yet they also learned new skills and developed talents that ultimately improved their ability to treat patients.

New Knowledge to Serve a New Nation

The Revolutionary War was a brutal and bloody conflict, but a few good things resulted from it. Perhaps the most important result was that the colonists finally won their freedom from Great Britain and joined to form the United States of America.

The war also benefited the medical profession in a variety of ways. Before the Revolution, some colonial doctors lacked hands-on experience. Doctors' high fees, as well as patients' fear of certain healing methods, limited the amount of time that doctors spent actually treating people. Doctors who had a formal education often knew about the latest advances in medicine, but they rarely had a chance to apply the new methods in day-to-day situations.

The Revolutionary War brought change for many physicians and surgeons. Colonists who served in the military medical unit faced a constant stream of patients coping with illness, injury, and life-or-death situations. These doctors had to think quickly and act fast. Several historians have noted that revolutionary doctors probably learned more by treating soldiers on the battlefield than they would have learned in any classroom or apprenticeship.

Medical experts who were part of the war effort also gained a new understanding of why it was important to show sympathy and compassion to their patients. Such doctors often dealt with people who were terrified, in pain, or struggling through the final moments of their lives. They learned how to listen to their patients and to offer them whatever comfort they could as the war played out around them.

Benjamin Rush lived from 1745 to 1813 and is remembered for his achievements as an American doctor and politician.

Some doctors, like Benjamin Rush, continued to improve the practice of medicine in America even after the war ended, in 1783. For a while, Rush had headed the Continental army's military medical unit. Once the war was over, he taught medicine at hospitals and universities throughout Pennsylvania. Though he still believed in ancient practices such as bleeding, he always urged his students and fellow doctors to research new methods of curing their patients. Rush also worked to benefit the mentally ill. For example, he encouraged the medical community to treat these patients with greater compassion.

Rush is a single example of the several individuals who shaped the role doctors played in colonial America. From Thomas Wotton of Jamestown to Benjamin Rush, people who practiced medicine during this period faced many challenges. Yet doctors also did a great deal to improve life for the colonists. Just as important, their profession—and how it was viewed—grew and changed along with America.

Glossary

amputations	surgical procedures in which extremites, such as arms or legs, are removed
anesthetics	drugs that cause a person to lose physical feeling in a certain part of the body
anatomy	the study of the human body
bacteria	tiny organisms that can cause infections
botany	the study of plants
clergymen	ministers and leaders in the Christian religion
Continental army	the army of the American colonists during the Revolutionary War
dysentery	a disease that causes severe stomach problems
emetics	medicines that cause someone to vomit
epidemic	a widespread outbreak of a disease
herbs	plants that are often used to make medicines and to add flavor to food
inoculating	exposing someone to a disease so that he or she develops resistance to it
leeches	bloodsucking worms
malaria	a disease that causes chills and fever and is spread by mosquitoes
regulate	to set standards that apply to fees or other professional requirements that define a certain trade or business
revolution	an organized overthrow of a government
smallpox	a disease that causes fever and skin blisters
sterilizing	destroying microorganisms in or on an object, usually by bringing it to a high temperature with steam, dry heat, or boiling
sweating	the process of causing someone's body temperature to rise in an effort to get him or her to sweat out impurities or excess bodily fluids

Find Out More

BOOKS

Kalman, Bobbie. *A Visual Dictionary of a Colonial Community*. New York: Crabtree Pub. Co., 2008.

Lange, Karen E., and Ira Block (photographer). *1607: A New Look at Jamestown*. Washington, DC: National Geographic, 2007.

Roberts, Russell. *Life in Colonial America*. Hockessin, DE: Mitchell Lane Publishers, 2008.

WEBSITES

ColonialHall.com—Benjamin Rush

www.colonialhall.com/rush/rush.php

Read a detailed biography of one of America's most famous colonial doctors.

Colonial Williamsburg—Life in the Eighteenth Century

www.history.org/kids/

Read more about colonial doctors' work, as well as the lack of modern scientific knowledge that limited it.

Colonial Williamsburg Kids—Medicine and Illness

www.williamsburgkids.com/people/illness.htm

Learn more about some of the herbs that colonial doctors commonly used to treat patients.

Index

Page numbers in **boldface** are illustrations.

About the Author

Katie Marsico has written more than sixty books for children and young adults. She lives with her husband and three children in a suburb of Chicago, Illinois.